W. W Rammsay

Sky Wonders

W. W Rammsay

Sky Wonders

ISBN/EAN: 9783337038724

Printed in Europe, USA, Canada, Australia, Japan

Cover: Foto ©Lupo / pixelio.de

More available books at **www.hansebooks.com**

SKY WONDERS

BY

W. W. RAMSAY, D.D.

BOSTON

LEE AND SHEPARD PUBLISHERS

10 MILK STREET

1893

PREFACE

I can lay claim to no other originality in this little volume than comes from a careful grouping of such scientific statements as have for years arrested my attention in the scholarly volumes of Rev. Dr. E. F. Burr, Bishop H. W. Warren, Dr. Samuel Kinns, Camille Flammarion, and Prof. Charles A. Young.

Hoping that it may brighten at least one hour of many a busy life, I cheerfully yield to a manifold request to give permanent form to material which has been so approvingly received from the platform.

W. W. RAMSAY

Boston November 1893

TO

The Rev. Louis Albert Banks, D.D.

WHOSE ENCOURAGING SUGGESTIONS
HAVE DONE MUCH TO GIVE PERMANENT
FORM TO THESE PAGES

THEY ARE GRATEFULLY DEDICATED

I

ROSE and poetry have vied with each other in efforts to interpret for us the mystic writing on the evening sky. Prosaic science has thoughtfully aided our comprehension by measuring and weighing those massive bodies, which in appropriate times sweep along symmetrical lines drawn for their circuits, while poetry employs every familiar symbol, that we may see the beauty and feel the majesty of the astounding realities which so wonderfully emblazon the canopy of night.

Longfellow is thinking of the flowery springtime :

Silently one by one, in the infinite meadows of
    heaven,
Blossomed the lovely stars, the forget-me-nots
    of the angels.

Baily has in mind acres of sparkling gems, as he writes of the

Stars
Which stand as thick as dew-drops on the
    fields of heaven.

Campbell sees a single star as it first comes to its place, when

The sentinel-stars set their watch in the sky.

It is of a beautiful constellation that Tennyson so sweetly sings :

Many a night I saw the Pleiades,
   Rising through the mellow shade,
Glitter like a swarm of fire-flies,
   Tangled in a silver braid.

But Derzhavin excels in metaphor appropriate in its brilliancy :

A million torches lighted by Thy hand
Wander unwearied through the blue abyss.
What shall we call them? Piles of crystal
   light —
A glorious company of golden streams —
Lamps of celestial ether burning bright —
Suns lighting systems with their joyous beams?
But Thou art to these, as the noon to night.

II

NE would not expect that any deep inspiration could come to the soul from the dark and silent night. But no canvas so appropriate for nature's most attractive picture as when

Night drew her sable curtain down
And pinned it with a star.

Nature offers many delightful compensations for the threatening frown which in the evening obscures the last ray of declining day. If for the first time we beheld the scene, we should echo a poet's tribute to the night:

A starry crown thy raven brow adorns;
An azure zone thy waist.

But for the lengthening and deepening shadows as the evening sun sinks to rest, we must remain unconscious of the peculiar wonders of the upper deep.

Only for the natural recurrence and familiar frequency of the display, we must affirm it the most attractive of all the splendors of the universe. At first only the most daring of the sentinel soldiers is seen to brave the hazard, and take a position so far from his fellows; but soon many companies follow,

Forever singing as they shine,
The hand that made us is divine.

The scene they illumine is more than enchanting, it is instructive and elevating, — for man is never so grand in mental achievement as when, like Kepler in his astronomical studies, he is " thinking the thoughts of God." These crystallized thoughts are sunken in infinite depths, where, kindled to an intense blaze, they disclose the presence of Him who calls them all by name, and leads them as a shepherd does his flock. Beautiful as is this blossoming field, its glory is greatly enhanced when the " pale empress of the night " bends her slender crescent on the western sky. And especially if, as sometimes occurs, there be seen striding across this dusky expanse the ominous comet, with its fragile train curved like an angel's cimeter on the overarching vault.

III

HESE varied objects have much in common, which entitles them to a common consideration. Their interesting faces are radiant with the same refulgent light. The investigation of light carries us back to the first creative day, when God said, " Light be," and light was. It flashes along the brow of the day, and the birds sing their matin songs. It shoots its splendid shafts into the homes of sleepers, and men arise to think and toil. It rests its crystal columns in valley depths, and spreads its sheen over mountain crests, and men call it day. It tints the flower, and causes the grass to grow. No wonder Milton in imaging the creative process, when, before the sun, light was "sphered in a radiant cloud," exclaimed with such rapturous greeting,

Hail, holy light, offspring of heaven, first-born.

Not only is the genial light so very beautiful, but it is full of insolubie mystery. Whence is it? What is it? How does it move? If Mercury with winged sandals was the fleet messenger of the gods, may we not appropriately regard the light as a worthy message-bearer to the outposts of widest spaces? Light is not the simple element we might imagine. The great Newton ascertained that fact, and was commendably curious to discover the number and nature of the primary colors. Patient research and intelligent experiment brought their reward, and the great fact was known if the strange mystery was not fully solved. Newton, however, was probably mistaken in regard to the nature of light. He thought that atomic particles were given off by the shining body, and these passing through space left its image on the eye of the beholder. This was the corpuscular theory. It, however, was abandoned by DesCartes and his disciples in favor of the undulatory theory, which teaches that certain vibrations have been imparted to the interstellar ether, and these waves bear an image to the sensitive eye. It is truly marvellous that the author of Genesis, so many ages before science had been formulated, wrote his history on the supposition of the undulatory theory, which is now generally held as true. Some well demonstrated assertions are of startling significance. Prof. Tyndall in his *Light and Electricity* informs us that of the red ray four hundred and seventy-four trillion four hundred and thirty-nine billion six hundred and eighty million of waves enter the eye in a second of time, and of the violet ray six hundred and ninety-nine trillion accomplish the same feat. Let us examine the significance of this unchallenged statement. In a year there are thirty-one million five hundred and fifty-seven thousand six hundred seconds. By counting three every second, a person could count ninety-four million six hundred and seventy-two thousand eight hundred in a year. Then to count the number of violet waves that enter the eye each second would require seven million three hundred and eighty-three thousand three hundred and thirty years. We do not challenge the fact, but make the computation to show how much it involves. It does, however, occur to us, that one, who in the name of the high priest of science could suggest anything so marvellous, ought not to have any difficulty in swallowing, at one effort, both Jonah and the whale.

We are not so much surprised at the rapid velocity of light, as that any one ever could have ascertained what it was. Nothing appears to have evaded the notice of those who observe for us the wonders of the sky. Galileo with his first telescope discovered four of Jupiter's moons, and was greatly interested to notice their revolutions around their planet. There are times when the earth is about one hundred and eighty five million of miles nearer Jupiter than at other times. So by comparing the time of a moon's emerging from behind the planet when the earth was nearest, and the time of the emergence of the same moon when the earth was farthest away, he of course had the number of minutes it would require the light to travel the intervening distance. Other methods of greater accuracy have confirmed the former results to be in the main correct. Now it is known that this messenger flashes through space at the rate of one hundred and eighty-six thousand three hundred and thirty miles a second.

There is strongest evidence that our earth and moon once shone by their own light. At such a time the earth would cast no shadow, and would endure no mention of a night. It would then be as hot at the poles as at the equator, and would know no change of seasons. Probably it was only when as a youthful prodigal it had squandered its resources, that it was willing to recognize the authority of the sun in ruling the day, and marking off the bands for the seasons. It was for this reason, probably, that an introduction of the sun to our earth was so long delayed.

IV

UT it is time we paid some attention to the wonders of our neighbors which float with us in the unbroken silence of illimitable space. It is rather natural to take a look at the nearest of these, since it is the one with which we are on very intimate relations. I refer, of course, to our moon, styled by Homer, "the silver-footed goddess." She attends us so faithfully, and compensates so largely for the absence of the king of day, that we are pleased to honor her majesty, and commend her to the acquaintance of her subjects. I fear some writers have taken liberties with the moon's reputation, since by Rabelais it is affirmed to have been made of green cheese. Nor was Scott quite at liberty to tell:

I saw the new moon late yestere'en
Wi' the auld moon in her arms.

Though, to speak the truth, this is a phenomenon to be observed every new moon. The light from the crescent shines on the earth, and is reflected back on the entire orb with force enough to show the outline of the dark portion, which thus appears to be in the arms of the new moon. Dekker, too, abused his privilege by saying he saw a man in the moon. In this he must have been mistaken, since there is neither air nor water on this satellite, which, of course, would make it impossible for human beings to live there.

Then, there was poor Burns with his facetious apology :

> The village ale had made me canty ;
> I nae was fou', but just had plenty ;
> The rising moon began to glower
> The distant Cumnock hills out-owre ;
> To count her horns wi' all my power
> I set mysel' ;
> But whether she had three or four
> I couldna tell.

It certainly ought not to be considered to the moon's prejudice that Burns was in temporary eclipse.

The moon's mean distance is nearly two hundred and thirty-nine thousand miles, which would be quite a bicycle trip, but is as nothing compared with the distances of most of the heavenly bodies. Opportunity has thus been afforded for close observation, which has been industriously employed, until the moon is almost as familiar to us as is the planet on which we live. On account of its numerous and lofty mountains, and its deep and deeply shaded valleys, it has amply repaid all the attention it has attracted. Mt. Blanc is our standard of supremacy, and we heartily endorse Byron's discriminating tribute :

Mt. Blanc is the monarch of mountains,
    They crowned him long ago,
On a throne of rocks, in a robe of cloud,
    With a diadem of snow.
About his waist were forests braced,
    And the javelin in his hand.
But ere it fall, that thundering ball,
    Must pause for thy command.

But on the moon are two-score mountains higher than Mt. Blanc. Some of them are higher than the Himalayas, while monster craters forty, fifty, and one exceeding a hundred miles across, indicate the terrible commotions that stirred its depths and scarred its surface in the long ago. We imagine some one has piqued the moon on its trifling proportions, for it has undertaken to get even by making trouble for the astronomers. The orbit is pulled and twisted, banged and battered, until about thirty irregularities must be regarded in mathematical calculations. The constancy of the moon is greatly to be commended. Those who dislike two-faced people will take no offence at this reliable satellite, for it has never turned but one face toward us. The period of its revolution on its axis is the same as the time of its revolution about the earth, which forbids our hoping ever to see the other side of the moon. One other influence of our nearest neighbor must not be forgotten:

The ocean, at the bidding of the moon,
Forever changes with the restless tide.

A great belt of water, made up of many waves, heaved high, and there held as though with some underlying support, is borne across the ocean, and is hurled in crested breakers on distant shores, as though in reckless sport the moon would show her power over the yielding wave.

As we reflect on what our moon is

to the earth, we ascertain with pleasure that all the planets except the inner two are attended by these interesting bodies, which, by reflecting back upon us through the night the light of the invisible sun, do much to render the darkness enjoyable as well as endurable. Mars has two such faithful attendants; Jupiter five, the last of which was discovered only a few months ago; Saturn eight; Uranus four; and Neptune one. If it be true as affirmed in mythology that Saturn has devoured some of his own children, we may wonder that eight still remain. One of these, Titan, is the largest moon in the solar system, being near four thousand miles in diameter, while ours is but two thousand one hundred and sixty-three miles. Even that, however, is sufficient to excite the jealousy of the quartette of Uranus, for their diameters range from about two hundred to five hundred miles. We are hardly reconciled to the fact that beautiful Venus should be without a satellite. So considered Frederick the Great, who thought it had one, and proposed naming it for his distinguished friend

Alembert, who, however, delicately declined the honor, pleading that he was not great enough to become the satellite of Venus in the heavens, nor well enough to be so on earth, from which we infer he was a bachelor; and then he added: "I know too well how small a place I occupy in this lower world to covet one in the sky." Possibly he may have heard of the recipe for cooking a rabbit, which began with the suggestion, "first catch him."

V

THERE are many influential bodies desirous of our acquaintance, but we cannot for that reason afford to keep our plainly apparelled neighbors waiting for recognition. So we must have a word to say about the planets.

These wanderers, as the general name implies, are not lawless vagrants, but may be found at any time just where regular habits in the past would warrant our looking for them. But being so much nearer us than the fixed stars, they are observed to change their relative positions, and for this reason are called by the name "wanderer." There are eight of these planets, which for variety in size, diversity of appearance, and peculiarities of condition are not surpassed, if, indeed, they are equalled by any stars in the dome of night. The planets with their attending moons form a large portion of the solar system. Our sun is at the centre of this system, from which place he sends his attractive power to all the planets, and these at the same time receive from him their light and heat. They, like their moons, are dark bodies, and shine by borrowed light. These planets are not exactly in the same plane, nor are they ever in range along any direct line from the sun. We, however, may, for convenience of illustration, imagine this, inasmuch as they never change their order of succession from the sun. Starting from this majestic centre we move out toward the most distant member of our system, but scarcely know where to make the first stop. Some astronomers have thought there were unmistakable indications of a small planet about eleven millions of miles from the sun; but better proof is wanted before we consent to halt there in our journey. Its existence, however, is predicated on an authority no less than the late Professor Watson, of the University of Michigan. Continuing our journey, we first come to Mercury at the mean distance of about thirty-six millions of miles from the sun. This is the smallest of the planets proper, being less than three thousand miles in diameter; but when favorably situated, it receives about seven times the amount of light that comes to the earth; so, though relatively small, it does considerable shining. Next we come to the orbit of Venus at a distance from the sun of about sixty-seven millions of miles. This planet is but little less than the earth's size; and when nearest us flames up with bewitching beauty. In classic times temples were dedicated to the goddess of love that was supposed to preside over the motions and phases of this neighborly orb. Then at the mean distance of about ninety-two and a half millions of miles we find our earth. Double this, and you have the diameter of its orbit about the sun. This number, one hundred and eighty-five millions of miles, will make for us a convenient "yard-stick" when we need to make some measurements in the sky. Hoping that earth will be reconciled to our temporary departure, we move straight along to a mean distance from the sun, of one hundred and forty-one millions of miles, which brings us to Mars. In August of 1892 we were at our nearest possible approach to this planet, and notwithstanding his being but little more

than half earth's diameter, he made a
most brilliant appearance, and in spite
of the reputation gained from his
flushed countenance, as being under
direction of the god of war, we found
him very peaceable, though but thirty-
five millions of miles away. Now we
pass over a wide interval before we
come to Jupiter, very appropriately
named for the king of the gods. Of
course mythology could do nothing
else, when it is known to be about
thirteen hundred times as large as the
earth. Though this kingly orb is
wheeling through space at a distance
of four hundred and eighty-three millions of miles from the sun, he receives
light enough to show one of the
grandest objects of the heavenly display. Dr. Young, of Princeton, to
whose latest work we have submitted
our figures for verification, says Jupiter
receives but one twenty-seventh as
much light and heat as come from the
sun to our earth, but as he is as large as
all the other planets combined, he still
holds his unchallenged place of supremacy. If, however, the theory be true that
he yet retains much of the heat which
belonged to his more youthful years,

he still has some light of his own, which greatly helps his shining.

It may be that the interesting belts about Jupiter are the remnants of such dense clouds as during the carboniferous age of the earth shut out the sun's rays, and thus prevented his introduction to our world until the fourth period of Genesis.

That he is cooling down so slowly is attributable to his great size, for all the bodies of our system that have not already become cold and dark are slowly changing into that condition. In this regard the earth is in a medium state between the moon and Jupiter. The moon's temperature is supposed to be at least two hundred degrees below zero, while we are happy to share a more endurable climate; and yet, causes are steadily operating which, after many ages, must bring us to the present condition of that old, burntout cinder. But as the race of men will certainly have become extinct before that distant day, it need cast no unwelcome shadow, nor send any apprehensive chill to those who now consider the probability.

VI

ASSING along toward outer space we come to the most wonderful planet of the solar system, Saturn. Its mean distance from the sun is about eight hundred and eighty-six millions of miles. Its volume is more than seven hundred times that of earth, so that even at that vast distance it has not been able to screen its existence under the mantle of night. The most beautiful feature of this planet is strangely unique, as there is nothing in all the sky which resembles its wonderful rings. There are three of these, one enclosing another, and all about the planet, from which, as well as from each other, they remain at the same distance. Their united breadth is, according to Sir John Herschel, about thirty-seven thousand miles, their thickness is about one hundred miles, and the diameter of the outer ring one hundred and sixty-eight thousand miles. The inner ring is about nine thousand miles from Saturn. When we remember that probably these rings are neither solid nor liquid, " but mere swarms of separate particles, each pursuing its own independent orbit about the planet," we may be astonished that they keep their places, though travelling with Saturn about the sun at the rate of five hundred and fourteen thousand miles a day. I wonder if these rings are destined to be changed into moons, or other satellites !

The next planet in order is Uranus, at a distance of eighteen hundred millions of miles from the sun. Notwithstanding it is more than sixty times the earth's bulk, it appears to the eye as a star of the sixth magnitude. Uranus, however, was unable to keep a secret. He doubtless supposed himself too far away from everywhere to be observed by any person. But not so. Thoughtful men noticed that in a certain part of his orbit, he showed a strong tendency to slip away into the darkness beyond, and yet the old sun would call him back to his place, and thus compel his reluctant obedience. Two wise men, guided possibly by their knowledge of human nature, suspicioned the existence of another planet still farther away, with which they imagined that Uranus was hobnobbing. On this narrow supposition, either being unknown to the other, they proceeded with their curious calculations, and though Adams first completed his work, LeVerrier soon followed, and wrote to Galle where to point his large telescope, and, strange to say, his intelligent expectations were fully realized ; for in that abyss, two thousand eight hundred millions of miles away, into which startling depth it requires the sun's light four hours and ten minutes to pierce, there was seen for the first time a vast world, one hundred and five times as large as our earth, silently sailing through his wide revolution of one hundred and sixty-four years. And this farthest planet in the solar system is named Neptune.

There is a curious proportion which, with the exception of Jupiter, all the planets observe in their distances from the sun. The space between Mars and Jupiter is nearly double what an observance of this law would have made it.

It was conjectured that an undiscovered planet was wandering in this space. Diligent search begun nearly one hundred years ago failed to find such a body ; but, strange to say, it has been rewarded by the discovery of one after another, until more than three hundred little worlds have swelled the curious list. The largest of these is named Vesta. Its diameter is about three hundred and twenty miles. With two exceptions, none of the others exceed one hundred miles in diameter, while many are probably but little more than ten miles from side to side. Speculation has been busy as to the origin of these planetoids or asteroids, as they are called. Some have thought they were the material which for want of the necessary cohesion failed to unite in one great body, and so adjusted itself in these numerous small orbs, which we find regularly travelling about the sun in a decidedly interesting and orderly way. Some wise men imagine that if Jupiter had attended to his own business without exercising his autocratic interference, this disunion never would have occurred ; but as these little worlds add so richly to the wonders of the sky, we are more than reconciled, we are contented.

VII

AT the centre of this vast system of whirling planets with their encircling rings and attending moons is our great sun. He is the most splendid object in the heavens, and whether we regard his immense size, his terrific tempests, or his brilliant countenance, we are compelled to award to the sun imperial honors. He claims to be eight hundred and sixty-six thousand miles in diameter and so would equal one and one-quarter millions of our earth. He is seven hundred and fifty times as large as all the rest of the solar system put together. Bishop Warren, in *Recreations in Astronomy*, assists our comprehension by asserting that if a hole were drilled down through the sun, from its north pole to its south, large enough to receive the earth, and if it were dropped to the bottom of this cavity, and others placed on top of this and each other, as a string of beads hanging perpendicularly, that one hundred and nine and one-half earths could thus be placed through the diameter of the sun. Some one has suggested that we imagine the interior of the sun scooped out as we might take out the insides of a pumpkin, leaving only the rind. Now, at the centre of this shell of the sun, place the earth with its moon as now at the distance of two hundred and thirty-nine thousand miles, and it would make its revolution without coming within one hundred and ninety thousand miles of this vast shell. Well, this old emperor needs to be wonderfully large to control such a vast realm as is under his rule !

On the sun's surface are great spots into which we might tumble our world, yes, or even the largest of the planets. Maybe these spots or dark places are great holes in the photosphere or gaseous envelope by which the solid part of the sun appears to be surrounded. There are terrible commotions in this photosphere, when, according to Dr. Burr, gaseous waves rush furiously together, and dash the hydrogen spray three hundred thousand miles into space.

VIII

N interesting inquiry is suggested here, as to how the sun renews its energy and replenishes its fires. One would imagine that even the heat our earth receives from the sun might soon exhaust the supply, and how much is our apprehension increased to learn that the earth receives but one part in two thousand million parts of what he furnishes to the planets, moons, asteroids, and empty spaces through which he is circling. It is thought that either or both of two means may be employed in replenishing this supply. One is by a constant and regular contraction of his volume. Helmholz considered that the shrinking of the sun's diameter by one ten-thousandth part would generate heat enough to compensate for the regular emission for two thousand years; and Professor Young suggests that a contraction of his diameter two hundred and fifty feet annually, would meet all demands now being made on our beneficent sun. The second method for keeping up the supply is by the falling of meteorites into the sun. Sir William Thomson calculated that if a body as large as Jupiter were to be attracted to the sun's surface, the impact would supply heat enough to last thirty-two thousand years. Surely between these two possible methods we are likely to be supplied as long as the most of us shall desire such conditions.

From Helmholz's theory above mentioned, it has been computed that the sun has been affording a constant supply of light and heat during at least eighteen millions of years, and it is also scientifically maintained that it cannot sustain life on our planet more than ten millions of years longer. These curious statements confirm the revelation that the present order of the heavenly bodies must sooner or later come to an end. ·

IX

OUR sun is only one of many millions of suns that come into the telescopic field. A careless observer would affirm that he beheld countless numbers of stars with the unaided eye, but it is certain that only about six thousand or seven thousand can be so observed in both the northern and southern hemispheres.

Owing to their different distances from us, the stars appear to shine with varied degrees of brightness. It is this fact that determines their magnitudes. The stars are divided into sixteen magnitudes, not determined, however, by their absolute size, but by their appearance to the unaided eye. Six of the largest of these divisions are visible without the telescope, while the other ten can only be seen by the aid of that instrument. Authors differ slightly in their estimates of the numbers in each. Approximately, of the first magnitude there are twenty; of the second, sixty-five; of the third, two hundred; of the fourth, four hundred; of the fifth, one thousand one hundred; and of the sixth, three thousand two hundred stars. Then the telescope, whose power brings the sun within two hundred thousand miles of the earth, finds millions upon millions of stars to be divided between the other ten magnitudes.

Charts of the heavens were made in very ancient times. It is said that of the sixty-seven constellations now found on celestial globes, forty-eight were familiar to Ptolemy, who was born about 70 A.D. Even Job, more than three thousand years ago, speaks of Orion, the Pleiades, with other familiar stars. The names of clusters of stars were arbitrarily given, although in some instances there is a fancied resemblance between the cluster and the object for which it was named. Some one says, the sky is nothing more than a menagerie. Though while many were named for beasts and birds, others were called for men, and harps, and ships.

Classic story has related some entertaining fables concerning many of the constellations. Ovid says the ancients counted seven stars in the Pleiades, but as one of them hid itself because of grief at the fall of Troy, we now see but six. Virgil says that jealousy caused Madame Juno to obtain from Thetis an order that Callisto and Boötes should never bathe in the ocean. Whether this story be true or false, certain it is the constellations mentioned always remain above the horizon, and so avoid the water as though afflicted with hydrophobia.

About the north pole are distributed several groups which, according to mythology, were active participants in an exciting drama. Cepheus to appease the anger of Neptune chained his daughter Andromeda, in sacrifice, to a rock on the Syrian coast. Young Perseus heard of it, leaped on Pegasus, and with Medusa's head in his hand, reached the victim just as she was about being attacked by the sea monster. The rescue was easy and complete. In commemoration of this event all the participants were assigned conspicuous places in the heavens.

All the stars we see in the sky belong to some constellation. As we shall see, they are moving with incredible speed, and yet to distinguish them from the planets they are called the fixed stars. When we become well acquainted with these great, bright orbs, we shall know, that fact is wonderfully stranger than fiction.

It is difficult to imagine them other than they seem, as from accustomed places they look down upon us every clear night. The beholder might be excused for thinking that those which seem near each other were in the same neighborhood. As Alcor nearly touches Mizar in the handle of the Dipper, they twinkle their pleasure at the deception, since they are really five thousand times one hundred and eighty-five million miles apart. It is interesting too, to observe how they are compelled to answer questions. Notwithstanding our old sun flares up at too great familiarity, astronomers have discovered more than twenty-five of earth's chemical elements in his structure. It will avail nothing for those monster orbs to rush into the dark like streaks of fire, for wise men are on their tracks, and will soon know them as intimately as they now understand the little moon, that tells so modestly the history of her early life.

X

ALL the stars we have mentioned, and all we ever saw, belong to a vast, dense ocean of suns, whose boundary extends so far that they lose their individuality in a mass of commingled light. It resembles a belt of fleecy cloud, which, extending below the horizon, and then round the earth, forms a girdle about the heavens. The ancients observed this great wonder and called it the path to the dwelling of the gods. Its dimensions are almost fabulous. Its general shape is that of a monster cheese. Its thickness is eight million times one hundred and eighty-five million miles. You remember we remarked that we should have use for that "yard-stick." But what of the *diameter* of this nebula? It is one hundred and seventy million times one hundred and eighty-five millions of miles. Let him fathom this who can! Light travels one hundred and eighty-six thousand miles a second. It requires eight minutes and twelve

seconds to come from the sun to us,
and four hours ten minutes to go from
the sun to Neptune. Now, how long
would it require to pass from side to
side of this vast nebula? Possibly
somewhere from twenty thousand to
thirty thousand years. Well may we
be amazed and wearied by our effort
to comprehend this statement. We
regard our sun as quite remote, and
yet its light reaches us in little more
than eight minutes. Now, how far
away, how sunken in the depths of
space, are the sentinels on the extremi-
ties of our nebula, when if one should
flash a signal to the other, twenty
thousand years or more would be required! But we must remember there
are about eighteen millions of stars in
the milky way. Our nearest neighbor
among them is more than thirteen
millions of millions miles away. It is
so remote that if we should represent
the distance of Neptune by *ten inches*,
our nearest star neighbor would be
one mile away. We need not marvel
that three years and eight months are
required for the transit of its flash
through this tenantless space. Alpha

Centauri is the name of this star, which is visible from the southern hemisphere only. If we should undertake to furnish room for all these eighteen millions of stars on a scale as liberal as this, it would truly demand magnificent distances.

Is our planning burdened to find room in the heavens for this one nebula, then how must we despair of accommodating all that are floating across the sky! Dr. Burr says they are found in great variety of beautiful forms. Some are round, others oval, or lens-shaped, or ring-shaped. One resembles a crab, another a fan, another an hour-glass, another a dumb-bell, another a whirlpool, and so on, exhausting almost every ideal form. Analogy would infer from the composition of the milky way that all nebulæ consist of stars in immense numbers and at tremendous distances. But this is questioned of many of those fleecy bodies, though some of them throw a spectrum on the screen which always indicates a solid body as its source. In which case, the nebulae would certainly consist of individual stars. As the wisest men can only speculate concerning the constitution of these curious masses, we leave them to the more definite revelations of the future.

Is it not probable that these numerous and inconceivably immense bodies are an extension of the harmonies of subordinate dependence and sympathetic motion, to the widest fields of space? Does not analogy need these ultimate masses to complete the ideal universe toward which we have been moving through the gradations of satellites, planets, suns, groups, and clusters? Do we imagine the orderly system to suddenly stop while on those upper fields thousands of scattered nebulae roam at will like unshepherded sheep? Rather may we not infer that our nebula is but one of a vast system of its kind, and that all are in orderly procession along great circular orbits, about some inconceivably distant centre, having for its perimeter outposts so far away that only an angel wing can span it without weariness, and only an angel eye can pierce it without terror!

XI

THE magnitude of our stellar system is apparent in a glance at Sirius, the brightest star in the firmament, whose light is twenty years in reaching us. Arcturus, so difficult to guide, sends his light to the earth in twenty-five years. The North star, which, as Shakespeare says,

> Of whose true fix'd and resting quality
> There is no fellow in the firmament,

dispatched forty-six years ago the light which arrived here last night. Then there are the beautiful Pleiades. Into what measureless depths are they sunken, from which their light, rushing on at the speed of one hundred and eighty-six thousand miles a second, requires seven hundred years in finding us ! The light which came to us last night from that pleasant constellation began its flight before America was discovered. Yes, and back of that, even before King John signed, at Runnymede, England's famous Magna

Charta. Think of all that has occurred
since then! Dynasties have risen and
fallen; empires have prospered and
crumbled, and still the tireless light
was approaching. It was not until
revolutionary changes brought by seven
centuries had occurred, that the time
for the bewildering journey had been
completed, and then, as we looked,
we beheld, near the zenith, the bright
court from which we joyfully received
this gayly caparisoned messenger. This
inconceivable space is sprinkled with
constant sentinels. Professor Ball, Royal
astronomer at Dublin, says: "We
may fairly take the numbers of stars
in the sky, *of the entire universe that
we see*, at one hundred millions." But
who can imagine the scene if the
famous Lick telescope were placed on
the most distant of these millions?
We should probably be on the verge
of another one hundred millions now
unseen — for here we observe but the
beginning of the Lord's ways.

It is because of this unimaginable
distance that the light of the six thousand multiple stars reaches us as the
light of single orbs. Some of these
are double, others triple, or quadruple.

That is, certain stars in the same relative neighborhood revolve about each other, or about a point in space as their centre of motion. Take the North star as an instance. It is a double star; and though it requires a good telescope to distinguish between the two, they are one hundred and five times one hundred and eighty-five millions of miles apart.

One would imagine that relationship at that distance had run completely out. But they manifest a decided attraction, and neither makes any motion without paying due consideration to the claims of the other. Often one star of such group is larger than the other, or others, in which case the larger star will take its place in the relative orbit of the smaller, which must now do some very rapid sailing to atone for its inferior size. If each is attended by worlds which are in their turn attended by moons, how numerous and complicated the circles and ellipses they would describe on the sky. How wonderful that the Creator should have had clearly in mind all these motions before a single orb had been launched on the upper deep !

XII

COMETS are to civilized people welcome visitors; but it was not always so. It is not many years since they were thought to presage famine, pestilence, or war, and threw nations into fearful terror and consternation. Cæsar's wife was greatly distressed, and would keep him away from the conspiring senate by telling him that a comet had been seen in the sky, and that,

When beggars die there are no comets seen.
The heavens themselves blaze forth the death
    of princes.

But since we learned that popes have such power over these monsters, we need fear no peril. You know it was in 1456 that Calixtus III. issued a bull against Halley's comet, which he imagined to be interfering in his fight against the Turks, and, like most people before Luther's day, it was obedient to his holiness, and — when ready, took its departure. These bodies, very pretentious in their style, swing through wide spaces, and support a brilliant train in their vast circuits. Very coquettish they are, for they sweep down near the sun, then away they go, taking their own time for returning. They maintain a provoking silence about themselves, though they have been compelled to answer certain questions in spite of their dashing efforts to get away. They are certainly very interesting bodies. They threaten often to brush us off our planet, and in 1861 we are said to have passed through the train of a comet; but the fact was unobserved by all save a few who noticed a slight electrical disturbance. It is probable that comets are of different densities, as they manifest varied appearances. Their constituent elements have never been accurately or definitely determined, though every additional opportunity for observation adds to our knowledge concerning these strange visitors. They have an extremely low density, as is shown by the fact that "small stars can be seen through the head of a comet one hundred thousand miles in diameter." Professor Young says a comet is probably composed of

small meteoric stones, widely separated
as pin-heads many feet apart, carrying
with them a certain quantity of envel-
oping gas. But if so, these meteorites
must be very small and widely separated, or they would not allow the eye
to pierce them through and through.

Sir John Herschel saw stars of the
sixteenth magnitude through Biela's
comet, though the nucleus and sur-
rounding coma were forty thousand
miles in diameter. Many persons in
1858 observed Arcturus through the
tail of Donati's comet, where it was
fifty-four thousand miles in thickness.
The train of the comet, however, is
not a permanent part of the body, but
consists of a stream of vaporous particles attending the comet in a direction opposite to the sun. Professor
Pierce thinks there must be five thousand million comets within the limits
of our system, of which more than five
hundred have been seen with the
naked eye. Some of these are quite
well known. Their diameters have
been calculated, their trains measured,
while the periods of their vast revolutions have been quite accurately determined. Some of the most noted in

our system, taken in regular order, are : Encke's, Biela's, Halley's, the comets of 1811 and 1680. Nor would we neglect to mention those known as 1844 and 1858. Encke's comet is claimed to have demonstrated that there is an interstellar ether. Halley's shows that it is possible to predict with certainty the revolution, which occupies about seventy-six years; while Biela's comet goes far toward identifying cometary matter with meteoric showers. Halley's has been traced back through Chinese history to the year 12 B.C. I presume the most beautiful comet my readers ever saw was Donati's, of 1858. Its train reached through forty degrees, while its head was two hundred and fifty thousand miles in diameter. It requires two thousand years for a single revolution. If astronomers can have three well-defined positions of a heavenly body, it enables them to give with surprising accuracy the nature, extent, and time of its revolution; or if its orbit be parabolic, they can encourage us to cast a lingering gaze, since the plumed knight will never return.

XIII

E are startled by the awful sweep of these thousand-year revolutions, but, we have entire respect for the statement. The comet of 1811 is a monster in size. Its head is one million two hundred thousand miles in diameter, while its tail reaches one hundred and thirty millions of miles into space. That is, it would reach from the earth to the sun and entirely around his majesty, with a flaming bow-knot. It visited the sun, when, according to Dr. Burr, our world was enveloped in the waters of the deluge, and then it disappeared, to be away in its ample revolution, for about four thousand years, which it completed in 1811, to again leave us for those wide, dark spaces of its wandering. The wonderful comet of 1680 has a mean distance from the sun of forty-four thousand millions of miles. Its train was a thing of beauty, stretching through seventy degrees of the sky. So, before the head of the comet had appeared above the horizon,

this flaming train had reached far beyond the zenith. What if we could
read the journal of this old traveller!
I think of it rushing down from its
flight of nine thousand years, to enjoy
the twelve thousand degree heat of our
great " natural furnace," and then, like
some mighty conqueror, adjusting his
great plume, beginning another fearful
flight into that far-away; but, O, who
can tell how far! Since 1680 it has
been dashing on at tremendous speed,
and still it goes. It will lean forward
in its outward flight for more than four
thousand years yet; still on and on,
until in those dark and cold spaces it
gently swings about the aphelion of its
orbit, and, like a proud athlete, rushes
down the unlit avenues to again re-
plenish its wasted brightness and de-
pleted energy at the central-fires of the
sun. Did we fail to follow the comet
for nine thousand years, then how
must we be lost in an effort to trace
the silent wandering of the comet of
1844? Its train was two hundred millions of miles long. Double the distance from here to the sun. How
beautiful to bend that splendid thing
of light on the distant sky; and then

begin his revolution, not of four thousand, nor nine thousand, but of one hundred thousand years! How strange that in that awful period he should all the while continue his allegiance to our little sun, and seek from mysterious distances communion with his attending worlds!

There is greater variety among comets than any other of the heavenly bodies. Some have several trains, others have none. The same comet at one appearance has one, while at the next it will have more than one, or none at all. They are identified rather by their orbits than by their appearances. Some thus have periodic times, while others are vagabonds, which make one voyage into our system and then sail away, without any promise of returning. Some are very orderly in their movements, while others allow themselves to be pulled about in a style anything but independent. Some remain for months in the telescopic field, while others hurry away, as though they were behind time. In fact, there is no view we can have of these splendid couriers which is not of entrancing interest.

XIV

E have delayed our reference to the comet Biela, that it might suggest to us another wonder in this interesting field. The comet Biela divided in two in sight of our earth, in the year 1846. Its time of revolution was about six and a half years, and after the division the two parts continued their journey in the old orbit and again appeared to us in 1852, about one and a half million miles apart; but when in 1859 they might again have been expected, they failed to appear and have never since been seen. The question is natural as to what has become of them. It has been quite clearly demonstrated that the old orbit of Biela is now the orbit of a sparsely sprinkled and very rare substance, which furnishes a diversified and pleasing entertainment in the ample sky. Almost any clear night, and especially in November, the beholder will be rewarded in watching for what are called shooting stars. These consist of a " little cloud of dust and intermingled gas." They generally fill an orbit through its whole extent, and thus revolve like a great band composed of millions of millions of small particles about the sun. I have seen it stated that more than four hundred such orbits have been definitely located. The earth passes through these orbits, or attracts some of their vapor to itself frequently. The numbers of meteoric particles which enter our atmosphere daily are estimated at more than ten millions. They may have been floating in undisturbed security for ages, but now, when for some reason they enter earth's atmosphere, they are set on fire by the friction, and consumed. It is but the work of a moment. They enter the atmosphere at about seventy-five miles from the earth, and disappear when about fifty miles away, and during this brief interval, flash, and are gone.

One of the most interesting of such rings of cometary matter is that through which our earth passes every August and November. The circumference of this orbit is about four thousand four hundred millions of miles, and what is very curious is, that in every thirty-third year the display becomes exceedingly gorgeous. It would be inferred that in one part of this orbit the small flecks are greatly more numerous than elsewhere, and when the earth enters this, as happens every thirty-three years, the display is fine beyond all expression. The length of this denser portion of the orbit is many millions of miles, and so continues the beautiful exhibition six hours or more. We may hope for this phenomenon in 1899. If we remember that so far from witnessing the burning of vast worlds, we are simply looking at the consumption of small particles of the trains that have not been able to keep up with comets in their rapid flights, and thus are sprinkled along the orbit through which they had come, we might fairly exult in the splendid spectacle. It is unfortunate for many of us that the display is finer toward morning, inasmuch as in the evening the meteors are following the earth, while in the later night, we are meeting them. It thus becomes probable that the comets are leaving fragments of their trains through all parts of space, or as in the instance of Biela's comet contribute nucleus and all to this brilliant destiny.

There is another class of bodies which fall out of the sky with great velocity, noise, and brilliancy. These are termed " aerolites," "bolides," "meteorites," or "meteoric stones." About two hundred and fifty have been picked up during this century, though only a few of these were seen to fall. The greater number are of stony structure, while a few are masses of iron, and others consist of both. There has been much speculation in reference to their origin. Some have thought they had been long ago ejected from the craters of the moon, and incidentally falling within the attraction of the earth, are brought to its surface. They are of irregular shape, which would indicate some such origin. The sun is supposed to be surrounded by myriads of them, and to use them for feeding his flames. Homer probably speaks of an aerolite, as he refers to Minerva's flight in the guise of a shooting star from Olympus. to break the truce between the Trojans and the Greeks.

XV

E had thought our sun was a very giant among the glorious galaxies of the sky; but what is our surprise to learn that he is far surpassed by some whose names and faces are quite familiar to us. If our great central orb were removed to the apparent *Ultima Thule*, where some of the former lord it over their kingdoms, his last ray of light would fade before completing its journey to earth. The brightness of Sirius is equal to sixty-three of our suns; the pole-star is as brilliant as eighty-six suns; but what of that? is not Capella equal to four hundred and thirty? is not Arcturus as bright as five hundred and sixteen? But what of that? is not modest Alcyone in the far-off Pleiades equal to twelve thousand of our sun? Whether Maedler was correct or not, in supposing that this famous star was the centre of all the suns, as in their majesty they bore about him their retinue of worlds with attending satellites, we may certainly agree that a twelve thousand fold sun could rise majestically to the needs of the sublime occasion. Certain it is that our luminary is passing, with his numerous dependents, through a wide orbit, and at last accounts was hopeful of accomplishing the revolution in twenty millions of our years.

Think of our following this fiery leader through spaces which, though apparently familiar, are ever new. We are this moment wheeling along a hundred millions of miles from where we were at the same hour yesterday, in a part of space we never visited before, nor shall we ever journey through it again. It is enough to make one homesick. Still on we go, but never able to overtake a single star in the firmament. We can never hope to float into the neighborhood of their massive proportions, and if we know of their density, size, and brightness, it is by the complex applications of scientific principles, from which even the stars cannot absolve themselves.

HE motions of the heavenly bodies are something startling. The whole heavens are in rapid transit. It may be that stars in any mentioned constellation do not move with the same velocity, and yet they are so far from us that the centuries do not serve to show any marked change in the figure of the Hyades, or Orion, or Cassiopea. Nor will we forget that there is great complexity of motion, since one system is carried about another, and both these are borne about a third, and these, without changing their motions as before noted, are still whirling without a jar around a more distant centre, until at the last the sky is full of this complicated network ; and yet somehow there are no detentions, no irregularities, no collisions. It is the complete harmony of the spheres, which was in God's great thought before He had as yet made a world, or fashioned a moon.

Our moon makes but small pretension to speed, but she completes her thirty-seven and a half miles a minute year by year. And then consider that it must keep up with the earth as it swings along at the almost incredible rate of nineteen miles a second. Not to forget that these must not be left behind as our sun with his giant servants is moving at the rate of four miles a second. We are astonished that nothing is disarranged or displaced on our planet during its fearfully rapid transit. Why does not this motion create an atmospheric current whose tornado-force would sweep every object from its surface? Simply because the earth carries its own atmosphere, which is as unruffled as the atmosphere of a parlor-car when the train rushes at the speed of fifty miles an hour. What in the realm of fiction is more wonderful than the velocity of Arcturus? It moves fifty-seven miles a second, that is three times as rapidly as the earth. And yet so far away is this five hundred and sixteen fold sun, that in a century it has changed its apparent place on the sky but three short inches! Who can comprehend the meaning of this statement, whose imagination can fathom the abysmal depth where this fearful flight is occurring? All astronomers make special mention of a star in the "Hunting Dogs," known as No. 1830 in Groombridge's catalogue of circumpolar stars. Its fearful velocity exceeds two hundred miles a second, which Bishop Warren affirms "is beyond what all the attraction of the matter of the universe could give it." But why need we wonder, for these are but parts of His ways; why marvel at this when many of the comets in their sweep about the sun rush at the inconceivable velocity of more than three hundred miles a second! We are awe-stricken and mute as these monstrous masses come bearing down toward us, then, like the whisk of an angel wing, they are gone, gone at the bidding and impelled by the power of Him whose they are and whom they serve.

As all these bodies are dashing about, around, and away, we can but resume our strange questionings concerning the terrible distances to which Heaven's bright messages are borne. Then with the fleshless spirit described by Richter, we cry out, "End of the universe, is there none?" We must long wait the answer. Men, in ancient times, with the unaided eye looked by night into heaven's rounded dome, and saw regiments of quiet stars twinkling from serene depths. Galileo then pointed his simple telescope into the same spaces, and there beyond the familiar fields he was entranced with the wonders of a new revelation. Then Lord Rosse, hopeful of yet richer discoveries, mounted a more powerful instrument for its still wider conquest, and sure enough, like beacons of brightness on crests of darkness, there were found myriads of sparkling worlds, far back in depths profound. Then we await tidings from the latest achievement in the renowned Lick telescope; and since the smaller magnitudes, because of greater distances, are vastly more numerous, we are bewildered to know that it pierces the hiding-places of double the number seen through the fine Washington refractor. And while we ask if there is no end to this universe, we are still unanswered.

Shall men ever know more than now about the boundaries of the sky? Why

not? Who has fixed limits to genius,
or waved mind back from the ampler
spaces into which the receding horizon
is beckoning it? It is but thirty-three
years since the spectroscope sent its
first challenge into the distant sky;
but it has rendered us familiar with
many properties, as if those orbs were
our nearest neighbors. Shall not other
mental possibilities evoke still stranger
truths from retreating worlds? The
discoverer's triumph is not to be mo-
nopolized by Galileo, or Herschel, or
Kirchhoff. They gave the world its al-
phabet of first principles, which distinguished scholars are busy combining
into strong chapters of sparkling truth.
Newton's sea-shell soliloquy is the na-
tive inspiration that shall certainly
extend the astronomer's vision out,
through, beyond, to where other myriads of burning suns glitter on the
farthest conceivable horizon.

XVII

WHO does not feel depressed as he looks from this un-bounded survey to his own little self ?

Fond man ! The vision of a moment made !
Dream of a dream, and shadow of a shade !

"When I consider the heavens, the work of Thy fingers, the m oon and star which Thou hast ordained, what is man that Thou art mindful of him, and the son of man that Thou visitest him?" But no, the giant stars are but toys for mind's delight, but lamps to light its way through the sky.

Space is but the expanse for mind's yachting excursions, while distant worlds are but convenient islands, where it anchors for temporary rest and recreation. Thought is the glory of mind. In a moment it spans the distance which only ages of light-travel could transcend. It holds aloft mon-ster balances, into which it tumbles giant worlds to determine their weight. It predicts the awful periods for widest revolutions. In its mighty and varied conquests it renders commonplace, mysteries which had once been reckoned first inconceivable, and then preposterous. Thought groups in a comprehensive system all the varied facts of the firmament, and thus presumes to interpret God's large handwriting on the crystal walls of the universe.

Mind with its consciousness, judgment, memory; with its responsibility, conscience, immortality, easily and immeasurably transcends the aggregate greatness of all worlds.

As Mrs. Hemans so sweetly sung:

> The sun is but a spark of fire,
>   A transient meteor in the sky,
> The soul, immortal as its sire,
>   Can never die.

Or we exult in the utterance of Philip Doddridge:

> Ye stars are but the shining dust
>   Of my divine abode;
> The pavement of those heavenly courts
>   Where I shall reign with God.

How truly the soul is winged for its immortal flight is beautifully expressed

in some lines from Moore's " Lalla
Rookh " :

> Go wing thy flight from star to star,
> From world to luminous world, as far
> As the universe spreads its flaming wall;
> Take all the pleasures of all the spheres,
> And multiply each through endless years,
> One minute of heaven is worth them all.

www.ingramcontent.com/pod-product-compliance
Lightning Source LLC
Chambersburg PA
CBHW021518090426
42739CB00007B/677